Ayr Memories

Jeanette Castle

KYLE & CARRICK DISTRICT COUNCIL

ERRATUM p42 picture no. 75
Caption should read -
St James' Parish Church, Newton-on-Ayr,1913. It became the
Parish Church for the North Newton congregation in 1904.

© Kyle & Carrick District Council
1994

ISBN 0 9511586 3 5

Published by
Kyle & Carrick District Council

Printed by
Cordfall Ltd
041 332 4640

Contents

Acknowledgements

I wish to express my appreciation to a number of people who have helped me in the production of this book:

Sheena Andrew who was a tremendous help in selecting photographs and checking facts; the staff of the Carnegie Library Reference Department for all their assistance and Charles Deas, who edited the book. Finally, I wish to thank my husband, Alan, for entertaining our son while I worked on this project.

Introduction

Much of the eight hundred years or so of Ayr's existence lingers on in the present in the Medieval layout of the streets. This book aims to take its readers on a stroll through some of the sights of Ayr. This is the second in a series of books depicting photographic memories of the towns of Kyle and Carrick. The first in the series was *Girvan Memories*, by James McMeikan (1993).

All the photographs in this book are held in the archives of Kyle and Carrick District Libraries. Individual photographs may be purchased through any library in Kyle and Carrick.

Below: This aerial view of Ayr, from about 1935 shows Ayr's bridges. From bottom to top: the Railway Bridge, built in 1909, but now demolished; the New Bridge (1879); the Auld Brig (c15th century and restored at the beginning of the century); Turner's Bridge (1900), Railway Viaduct with pedestrian walkway (1880s), Victoria Bridge (1898).

Townhead

2. Burns Statute Square. The poet looks toward his birthplace in Alloway. In earlier times, this was the site of the Cattle Market. Before that it had been the farming land of the Burgesses of Ayr.

3. The ironwork which is visible here was removed during the Second World War.

4. Burns Statue Square, showing the Temperance Hotel, 1892.

5. The unveiling of the statue of Burns by Sir Archibald Campbell (Lord Blythswood), Grand Master of Scotland, on 8th July, 1891. Ayr Burns Club had gathered together 450 people to form a Burns Choir to raise money for the raising of a statue to Burns.

6. The Royal Scots Fusiliers Memorial, Burns Statue Square. This monument was unveiled in November, 1902. The Fusiliers, the County regiment of Ayrshire since 1873 had fought in the Zulu War of 1879, the Transvaal Campaign of 1880; Burma, 1886 and in the Boer War, 1899-1902. The Regiment lost many men in the Battle of Spion Kop, January 1900, an event remembered in a nickname given by local people to a tenement in King Street.

7.

7. Alloway Street is depicted in the following four photographs showing the changes over a period of 25 years. There were many changes in this area after the opening of the new railway station. The street was widened and elegant shops appeared. This 1903 photograph shows the area soon to be developed.

8. This photograph shows Alloway Street again, but in 1905.

8.

9. This area was known as the Cowgait early in the town's history. It was where the Burgesses pastured their cattle.

10. The old and the new. A horse and cart alongside a tram. The trams ran from 1901 until 1931. The first track stretched from Prestwick Cross to St. Leonard's Church. In 1902, the line was extended to Burns Monument in Alloway, passing the Old Racecourse. In 1913, a branch line was built from the New Bridge, along River Street to Wallacetown and Hawkhill to serve the new racecourse which had opened in 1907.

High Street and Sandgate

11. Tam O'Shanter Inn. This famous High Street landmark took its name in the 1840s in order to attract tourists passing up the High Street from the railway station, then at Newton, on their way to Alloway. It traded as a public house until it was bought over by the Burgh of Ayr in 1942. It operated as a museum from 1957 until 1988. In 1993, it reopened as a public house and restaurant.

11

12. The sign above the door indicates that A. Glass was the publican. The thatched roofs are clearly visible.

13. Tam O'Shanter Inn, c1904. The shop styles are beginning to change with the gradual removal of one storey gable ended buildings.

14. High Street, c1860, from Townhead. Many of the 18th century buildings shown here were soon to be replaced.

15. This view from the late 19th century, shows a more bustling scene and some fine examples of the costume at the time.

16. A view of the High Street just before the introduction of the trams.

17. The trams were an established form of transport by the time this photograph was taken in 1909.

18. The High Street in the 1930s. The trams have gone, leaving the road free for the motor car. The Wallace Tower, which dominates the scene had been built in 1834 replacing an earlier tower which had stood on this site. That had been the Town House of the Wallaces of Shewalton. Until the 1840s, people had to walk around the tower and not under it. A hall was added in the 1880s.

19. Carrick Street in 1930. Originally known as the Carrick Vennel, this was the route from Ayr to the Burgh Moor, Alloway and the River Doon. In the 1850s, Carrick Street was the location for a School of Industry, supported by the Earl of Eglington. A Church of Scotland Mission Hall was built in 1868.

20. The High Street has, at varying times, been known as Cammergate, Marketgate, Main Street and King's Street.

21. While the trams may have gone, there are still some remains even today. Brackets on the walls of some of the buildings in the town centre can still be seen.

22. The site of the market. The Bank of Scotland building stands on the site of the Wool Market and the Web Market. Ayr had been involved in cloth trading since before 1560. British Home Stores stands on the site of the Franciscan Friary (the Greyfriars), established in 1474. Remains were uncovered during excavations before the building of the present shop in 1982. BHS retains its red sandstone Victorian frontage.

23. Lorne Arcade, 1903; showing the covered arcade which still exists.

24. Ayr Auld Kirk is reached by passing through the 'Kirk Port' from the High Street. The Auld Kirk was built between 1653 and 1655 with compensation money from the government, after Oliver Cromwell had constructed a 'fort' or 'Citadel' which enclosed the Kirk of St John the Baptist. The first minister was William Adair whose statue stands beside the Church. The Kirkyard contains a memorial to the Covenantors as well as graves of friends and contemporaries of Robert Burns. A Lych Gate, containing two mort safes from 1816, guards the entrance. Mort safes were supposed to prevent body snatching!

25. An illustration depicting the Fish Cross in 1814. This marked the north end of the market area. This area was the centre of the town's business activity. It was here that some of the proclamations were read out. The selling of fish was banned here in 1853 but the name, Fish Cross, remained.

26. Fish Cross, 1903; showing the width of the street where the market area began.

27. High Street, 1910. The oldest part of the town. Many of the town's inhabitants in the 17th century had their own private wharves behind their houses.

28. This corner of the High Street leads from the Fish Cross and the 'Back O' the Isle'. In earlier times this area resembled the Shambles in York with its overhanging buildings. Visible in this photograph are a bookshop 'Lorie's Library' and a chemist's 'Graham & Primrose'.

29. High Street, in the 1920s, showing the Town Buildings on the right. Tram No. 18 was often decorated on special occasions. Tram No. 28 had been bought from Manchester Corporation.

30. Sandgate, c1887. The steeple of the Town Buildings is c225ft high and was built in the late 1820s. It was designed by Thomas Hamilton, who also designed the Wallace Tower and Burns' Monument. The Town Hall was not added until the 1880s.

31. Sandgate, 1906. The building with the crow-stepped gables and steep-pitched roof dates from the early 1600s. It is known as Lady Cathcart's house. The Cathcarts were a prominent local family who acquired this Town House in the mid-18th century. In 1991, restoration work, undertaken by the Scottish Historic Buildings Trust, began on this property after it came close to being demolished.

32. Sandgate, 1907, looking north. In the background, the familiar outline of the Carnegie Library, opened in 1893, is clearly visible.

33. Sandgate, c1890. Note the boys without shoes.

34. The building on the right, just before the street narrows, was the County Club Building for Gentlemen.

35. Sandgate, from the Malt Cross, in the 1940s. In the 1400s, this area suffered from the problem of sand being blown onto it. In 1425, a Royal Order was issued to narrow and straighten the Sandgate.

36. The premises of J. Mackie, Motor Hirer, stood on the site of the new Fire Station in the Sandgate (opened 1930).

37. Newmarket Street, 1890. The buildings in this street date from the 1820s. This street was previously known as Trinity Vennel. In 1767, it connected the Sandgate to the new Butter and Cheese Market. On the left of this photograph stands the McNeille Buildings built 1869-1870. It was named after John McNeille who was Provost of Ayr between 1864 and 1873. A public library was opened here in 1870. On the entrance to this building can be seen the sculptured heads of Robert the Bruce, Sir William Wallace and John Knox.

38. Newmarket Street, 1885. On the left stands the Post Office. Other businesses in the street were: no.47 John Brown (Baker); no.49 Mr J. Bell (Wool Shop); no.51 James Caw (Glass and China); no.44 John MacLeod (Painter); no.46 James A. Morris (Architect); and no.50 L. Le Clair (French hairdresser).

The Auld and New Brigs

39. Auld Brig, 1894.

40. Auld Brig, 1900. These photographs were taken before the restoration of this fine historic bridge. From the 15th century, this was the entry point into Ayr from the North. It replaced a wooden bridge.

41. Auld Brig, 1907. By 1905, the bridge had deteriorated to such an extent that pedestrians had to be prevented from using it. A campaign to restore the bridge was led by James A. Morris, a prominent local architect. Also involved in the campaign were Lord Roseberry and R.A. Oswald of Auchincruive. Work began in 1907.

42. The triumphant Restoration Committee on the restored bridge in 1910.

43. The first New Bridge was built in 1787 but was severely damaged by flood in 1877. The ornate statues now stand in the gardens at Burns Monument while some of the balustrades surround the Pavilion on Ayr seafront.

Reproduced with permission from the George Washington Wilson Collection, Aberdeen University Library

44. The second New Bridge, c1890. This bridge was built in 1878 at a cost of £15,000.

45. Nether Mill, 1900. The dam incorporated cruives (fish steps) to allow salmon to pass through the dam.

The Harbour

46

46. An atmospheric picture of 1860. The Town Steeple and the first New Bridge can be clearly seen. Notice the sailors clothes hanging out to dry on the rigging of the ship.

47. The harbour was extensively developed between 1874 and 1881 with the construction of a wet dock and a slip dock.

48. The harbour, c1890. mining, agriculture, industrialisation and the railway boom all contributed to the growth of the harbour.

49. This 1905 scene shows some of the extensive warehouses which surrounded the harbour area. Imports included salt, grain, yarn, limestone, slates, timber and whisky. Exports included coal, agricultural products and pig-iron.

50. 1910. By this time, the brisk trade with Liverpool, had all but died out.

51. Harbour, 1910, showing the industrial activity on the Newton side of the Harbour.

52. The Harbour again from around 1910. After this date, the harbour began to encounter financial problems resulting in the Railway Company taking over the operation of the harbour in 1919. From 1950, the harbour was managed by the Docks and Inland Waterways Executive.

The Road to Wellington Square

53. South Harbour Street, c1904 with its warehouses and Miller's Folly, named after John Miller (Baron Miller) who lived at St John's Tower.

54. This view also from around 1904, shows Loudoun Hall behind the white building. Although the wing to the left has been demolished, the remainder of the Hall has been restored. Loudoun Hall was built for James Tait, a Burgess of Ayr at the end of the 15th century. It is Ayr's oldest house.

55. Ayr Academy, 1890, before the extensions were built. The Academy has a long history. There are references to the School of Ayr from 1233. The present school was built in 1880.

56. The Academy with the extension designed by James A. Morris in 1912. There are three sculptured heads on the building: Wilkie, representing art; Burns, representing literature and Watt, representing science.

57. Mr Laurence Anderson, (Art Master) at Ayr Academy, with an attentive class c1890.

58. During the First World War, Ayr Academy staff and pupils contributed to the war effort through fund raising ventures. Raising money to pay for beds in military hospitals was one of their efforts.

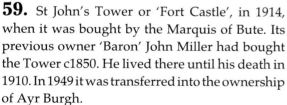

59. St John's Tower or 'Fort Castle', in 1914, when it was bought by the Marquis of Bute. Its previous owner 'Baron' John Miller had bought the Tower c1850. He lived there until his death in 1910. In 1949 it was transferred into the ownership of Ayr Burgh.

60. The Church of St John the Baptist was built in the 12th century and was in use until the 1690s. The Tower was a 14th century addition. The Church and Tower were enclosed in Oliver Cromwell's Citadel in the 1650s when the church was used as an armoury.

61. Wellington Square began to be laid out in 1808 and acquired its name after Wellington's victory at Waterloo. The War Memorial to the dead of the First World War was unveiled in 1924.

62. The Proclamation of the new King, George V at the County Buildings, May 1910. The County Buildings, built in classical style in 1825, were designed by Robert Wallace.

63 & 64. The Territorial Review of 8th June, 1912.

63

64

65. The Stevens Fountain on the Esplanade dates from 1892. It was gifted to the town of Ayr by Hugh Stevens, a Glasgow ironfounder who lived in Skeldon House, near Dalrymple.

66. Behind the Stevens Fountain is the forbidding Gaol designed by Robert Wallace and opened in 1823. It was closed down in 1931.

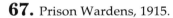

67. Prison Wardens, 1915.

Down to the Seaside

68. The Pavilion built in 1911, was designed by James K. Hunter of Ayr, a former partner of James A. Morris. Ben Popplewell's summer shows ran here from 1913.

69. The Bandstand on the Low Green, 1910. A football match was held here in 1887 to raise funds to build the Bandstand.

70. Ayr Beach, 1905. Attractions on the beach at that time included pony rides, boating, band concerts and ice cream vendors.

71. Bathing machines were introduced by the town Council's Attractions Committee in 1902. It is interesting to see how modesty prevailed with one bathing machine well into the sea.

72. A crowded Esplanade, 1928. The Pavilion hosted many entertainments for the visitor.

73. Boating Pond and Esplanade, 1940.

BOATING POND AND ESPLANADE, AYR.

Newton Sights

74. The Carnegie Library opened to the public on 2nd September, 1893. Inside, there is a fine stained glass window designed by Stephen Adam and Co., Glasgow.

75. St John's Parish Church, Newton-on-Ayr, 1913. It had became the Parish Church for the North Newton congregation in 1904.

76. The Main Street of Newton in the early years of this century. Newton was a burgh in its own right until 1873 when it had become part of Ayr.

77. Prestwick Road, from Tam's Brig, c1910.

78. Garden Street behind the Carnegie Library.

Residential Glimpses

79

79. The Putting Green on the Esplanade, c1925. The Gas Works, originally built in 1826, were removed in the 1960s.

80. The Ayr County Motor Company, Dalblair Road, c1911.

81. An advertisement from the Ayr Directory, 1906-7.

80

82. Racecourse Road, 1908. This area saw a rapid growth in villa building in the second half of the 19th century. A municipal golf course was built in this area when the new racecourse was opened in 1907 near Craigie Park.

83. The Seatower Hotel, Racecourse Road, c1900. It was built in the 1860s in Scots baronial style.

84. Dalblair Hotel, c1924. The original Dalblair House had been built in the 1770s for James Gibb, an Ayr soap manufacturer.

85. Belleisle House, c1930. Hugh Hamilton of Pinmore built the mansion house after acquiring the estate in 1787. Ayr Burgh took ownership of the estate in 1926.

Alloway & Burns Memories

86.

86. Mrs McNicol's Tea Rooms on Mains Hill were a welcome stop for those walking out to Alloway to visit Burns Cottage and Monument at the end of the last century.

87. Alloway Railway Station opened in 1906 on the coast line from Ayr to Dunure and on to the new Turnberry Hotel which was built by the Glasgow and South Western Railway.

87.

88. Burns Cottage, Alloway, 1918, showing the tram approaching from Ayr. The Cottage had been used as an inn by the Incorporation of Shoemakers until it was purchased by the Trustees of Burns Monument in 1881. A museum was added in 1900.

89. Burns Gardens, Auld Brig O'Doon Hotel and Burns Monument Hotel, 1929. The gardens behind the hotel were created by David Auld of Doonbrae, the first custodian of the Burns Monument. The hotel dates from 1829.

90. Burns Monument, 1921. Designed by Thomas Hamilton in 1818 and completed in 1823. The Hexagon museum was added in 1830.

The Tramways

91. Ayr Corporation Tramways ran cars from Prestwick Cross to Alloway from 1901 to 1931. A branch line to serve the new racecourse opened in 1913.

92. Opening of the Ayr Tramways, 26th September, 1901. Provost Templeton drove the first tram over the New Bridge to inaugurate the service.

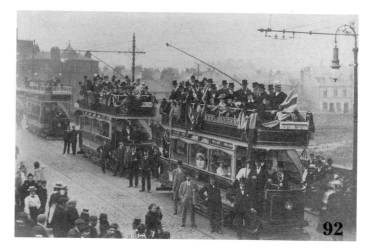

93. Tram depot staff at Newton Park pose in front of an open topped tram and a covered tram.

Ayr People at Work and Play

94. A winter scene at Castlehill Pond, c1907.

95. River Ayr, c1925: The ladies are walking along the path beside the river at Wallace's Heel and the Lime Kiln. William Wallace is reputed to have left an imprint of his foot on this bank of the river when escaping from an English attack. The Lime Kiln was worked here from around 1750.

DOONFOOT, AYR.

89227

96

96. The River Doon at Doonfoot, c1932. Doonfoot Mill can be seen on the far shore. Doonfoot, Alloway and Whitletts were all incorporated into Ayr Burgh in 1935.

97 & 98. Stepping Stones at Overmill, 1910. A mill is recorded on this site in 1594. The last mill here was demolished in 1963 during the construction of the Ayr by-pass.

99 & 100. The Ayr Show, 1893. Organised by the Ayrshire Agricultural Association, the show was first held in Beresford Park. In 1896 it moved to Dam Park which had been bought by the Association.

101. The New Racecourse, 1907. People came from all over the country to race meetings in May, July, August and September.

102. Ayr Racecourse, 1915. During the First World War, a Training Unit of the Royal Flying Corps was stationed here.

103. The staff of the Viewfield Laundry in Allison Street, c1920.

104. An advertisement for Viewfield Laundry showing the wide area covered by its agents.

105. Girdwood's Bakery staff, c1900.

106. Ayrshire Yeomanry outside Alexander's Stores, Alloway Street, c1905.

107. This ornate Roller Skating Rink at Boswell Park became the Picturedrome before 1914. During the first World War, a recreation area inside the Picturedrome was set aside for soldiers and sailors stationed in Ayr. In 1922 it was reconstructed as the Playhouse. It burned down in 1929. Green's Playhouse was built on the site in 1930.

108. Jean Miguet is pictured here on Ayr Beach, c1930, with the aircraft he designed himself, Le Pou de Ciel (Flying Flea).

108

109. Ayr Industrial School Band. The School of Industry descended from the Ragged Schools for Unfortunate Children in 1874. These schools were located next to St. Leonard's Church at 'Commonhead'.

110. Charlie Kemple's Super Entertainers appeared at Ayr Pavilion during the summer season of 1926. The group is pictured here with Leslie and Eric Popplewell. The Popplewells ran the Pavilion from 1913 to 1918 and from 1922 to 1967. The Popplewells also operated Ayr's Gaiety Theatre from 1925 until 1972.

111. Jack Belton's Ayr Entertainers, on stage in 1908.

Map

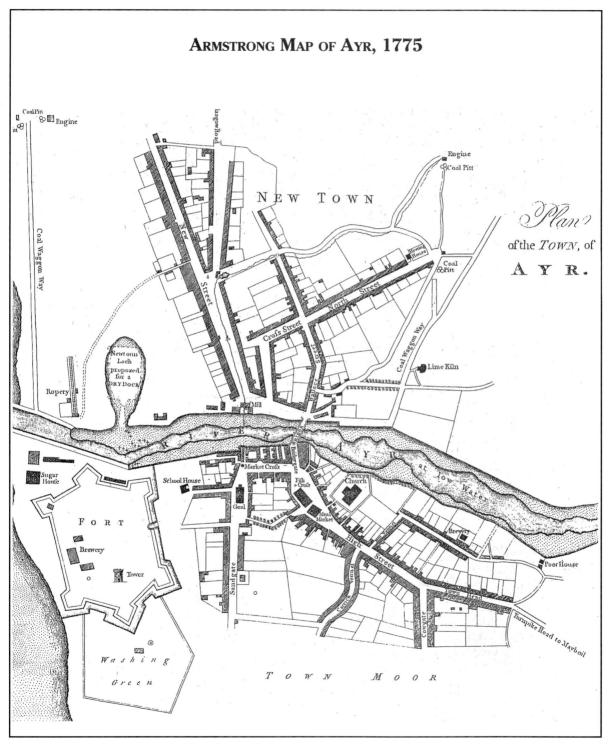

ARMSTRONG MAP OF AYR, 1775